# THE
# What if?
## BOOK OF QUESTIONS

to some of *your* most
revealing answers on

## LOVE and HEALTH
## WEALTH &
## HAPPINESS

Published by
Easton Studio Press
P.O. Box 3131
Westport, CT 06880
(203) 454-4454
www.eastonsp.com

Book and cover design by Miggs Burroughs
www.miggsb.com • Twitter @miggsb

Paperback ISBN: 978-1-935212-88-1
E-book ISBN: 978-1-935212-87-4

First edition
Printed in the United States of America
First printing: August 2012

This odd little book
is dedicated to
everyone out there
searching for questions
to go with their own
weird and wonderful
answers.

What if the most important moment in your life is this one? Can you handle the power it gives you to choose how you will spend the next one?

What if choosing to
read this page at this
moment is also a choice
*not* to stand on your
head, go to France or do
a million other things?
How many choices
does a person need?

What if you are in
an undesireable
relationship or
situation right now?
How many positive
steps have you chosen
not to take today?

What if everyone in the world was really a piece of you in disguise – the angry you, polite you, black, white, smart, stupid, young & old you. How many do you recognize?

What if someone else
has everything you
think you need to be
happy. How close do you
have to be to these
things to be content?

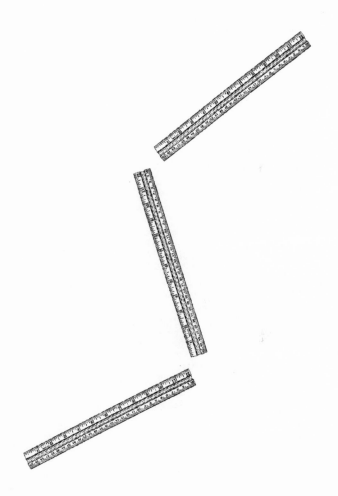

What if you were a plant, covered with leaves, thorns, roots, bugs and dirt. Could you accept *everything* that goes with being a plant?

What if you let go of
all the definitions and
judgements that
imprison you?
How free could you be?

What if your
thoughts and values
suddenly appeared as
pictures all over
your body? Would you
stay inside or go to
the beach?

What if The Truth is
made up of all the lies
owned by each of us?
How many do you
still hold onto?

What if you were to
write an ad for the
story of your life?
Would it be full
of hype or hope?

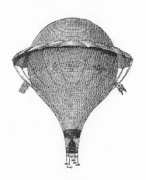

What if you were to find something on the next page offensive? How much responsibility are you willing to take for that?

What if the same
illusion of ownership
that connects you to
what you have,
can connect you
to what you want?

What if you were the
last person on earth.
Who's the only person
left to make you feel
loved… and why
wait to be the last
person on earth?

What if you have only
one more day to create
a positive change in
your life? What are
you waiting for?

What if, when you die,
you go to the same
place you were before
you were born.
Can you live with that?

What if you found out
that the person who
wrote these questions
is an ugly disagreeable
creature? Will your
answers change?

What if you were a
nasty little weed
sprouting right in
the middle of
a lush, green lawn?
Do you have a
right to be there?
Does the lawn?

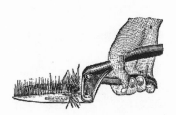

What if you spend
most of your life
struggling to achieve
some lofty goal. How
much is "most of your
life" worth when
it's all over.

What if your body
was actually just a
suit that you could
remove at any time.
Do you like the person
who's been hiding
inside?

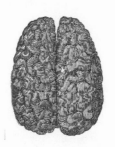

What if I played the piano while you dug a ditch? Would there be any music in your digging or any ditch digging in my music?

What if the best way
to enjoy your life is to
welcome whatever it
has to offer? Are your
heart and your
arms open?

What if you were to sit
on the moon watching
the rest of us bustling
around on earth. What
would love, happiness
and trust look like
from there?

What if you think of
all the things you need
to feel fulfilled. Who is
the only one with the
magic to make it
all happen?

What if you insist on
defining whats
beautiful or not?
Should trees or
spiders or children or
worms pay attention?

What if ten years
from now, you're
granted a wish to be
ten years younger?
How desireable would
this age be now?

What if you were to pay
$50 for a pair of shoes
and a tomatoe?
Does your wallet really
care if the shoes were
$1 and the tomatoe
was $49?

What if you give
yourself a gift today
and every day?
Do you deserve
any less?

What if you could
experience one nice
moment each day?
Couldn't you have a
nice life this way?

What if fear, anger, envy and insecurity are part of your wardrobe? Why do you insist on wearing the same thing every day?

What if someone you care about vanishes. Are they any further from your heart than if they were standing behind you.

What if the only
thing you can truly
own is a thought?
Is there anything you
can't have; anywhere
you can't be?

What if you could see
the path from today to
tomorrow as clearly as
you can see the path
from yesterday
to today?
Where are you going?

What if you made a list
of all the things you
don't have, like love,
health or wealth?
Are these things really
missing from your life,
or are you missing
from theirs?

What if the sure way
to find out what you
are really guilty of is to
make a note of every-
thing you blame on
everyone else?

What if all the
words and numbers
disappeared from
books, clocks,
calendars and maps?
Who will decide who
and what and where
you are right now?

What if you are
a gift to the rest
of us on earth?
When will you be
ready to accept
that fact?

What if rain ruins your picnic but feeds the plants, and the wind takes your hat but clears the fog? Can you be happy in a crazy place like this?

What if you are ready
to believe the worst
about yourself? What
are the rest of us
supposed to believe?

What if you make a list of everything you have and another list of everything that's missing? Which list describes you best?

What if hurting, leaving and ending are just mirror images of healing, arriving and starting. Have you looked in a mirror today?

What if you were to
step outside and accept
a bird or a tree for
exactly what it is?
Why not let the birds
and trees do the
same for you?

What if the next time
you go dancing you
pretend there's nobody
watching? What kind
of dancer could you be?

# What if this page doesn't page doesn't meet your expectations?

**What do your expectations have to do with what this page wants to look like?**

What if later today
you find everything
you are looking for?
What will you look
for tomorrow?

What if you laugh at
the next thing that
scares you? Is that
what fear sounds like?

What if certain people or topics make you furious. What part of you is that anger trying to erase?

What if you took a
minute or two to
reassure someone you
know that they
make a difference?
Why not practice
on yourself?

What if things don't go
your way today? Can
you make your way go
the way things are?

What if you were
a bird that didn't
believe in water?
Should fish stop
swimming?

What if you were to welcome all aspects of your personality into the "club" that is you? If you don't, who will?

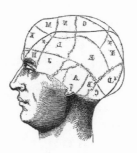

101

What if certain people
make you feel guilty
or angry or worthless.
Who gave them this
awesome power – and
who can take it away?

What if leaving is
just the first step to
arriving? Where are
you headed now?

What if you could
watch a movie of every
single moment of
your life? How many
did you really
bother to direct?

What if there were no
words for hot and cold,
happy and sad, rich and
poor, pain & pleasure?
Who will define
how you feel?

What if you behaved just like you were confident, caring and happy with what you have in life? What would people think?

What if, in the eyes
of a potatoe or
a butterfly or a cloud,
you have every right to
be exactly who you are.
Do you need more
approval than that?

What if all ads, book covers, packaging, and commercials disappeared? Who will decide what you really need to get through the day?

What if you run away
from everyone and
everything in a dream?
How far away from it all
would you really be even
if it wasn't a dream?

What if your
greatest weakness is
just your greatest
strength in training?
Have you worked
out today?

What if the next
person you meet has
lost all faith in
humanity? Would
they feel differently
if "humanity"
was you?

What if it's really the spaces between the spokes of your life that are holding your wheels together. When is the last time you looked between the spokes?

What if you measured
the success of each day
by what you gave
instead of by what
you got? Has the
meter moved yet?

What if after reading this book, you unlock one brand new, positive thought? Who put the lock on those thoughts in the first place?

What if you collect the
moments of your life
like beads on a string.
How much valuable
string are you using
up with small
colorless beads?

What if everything
you feel towards
someone else is just a
reaction to that piece
of you disguised
as them?

What if you had the power to make people glad to see you where ever you go? When will you start using it?

What if there was
absolutely nothing
missing from your life.
Would what you have
fill a basket or a
warehouse?

What if you were a river. Would you want boats floating gently with the tide, or lunging and lurching against your every ripple and bend.

What if the next time you feel guilty, happy, angry or worthy, you take all the credit. Is there anyone else writing your book?

What if you put this
book on a table and
left the room.
Do the questions
vanish because
you do?

What if the best way
to be heard is to stop
talking? Have you
listened to what your
heart has to say, lately?

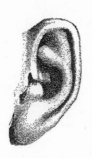

What if someone steals
everything you own?
What's left – the
poverty of needing
more, or the wealth
of needing less?

What if turning
this page could
create a positive
change in your life?
Is it possible to be a
victim with this
kind of power?

What if the person who professed their love for you yesterday betrays you today? Are they allowed to direct their own movie?

What if you really are
as smart & stupid,
selfish & generous,
strange & normal as
everyone thinks?
Where do you look
for the truth?

What if your personality
is like a hook, waiting for
someone to hang up their
love and attention.
How about learning to
love your hook just
the way it is?

What if you wake up
with no country, job,
partner or religion?
Who are you without
these things.

What if you look at
every dream, sneeze,
blister, person, accident
and cloud as a gift?.
Could you buy
anything better?

What if the only betrayal or anger or selfishness you can ever know, is your own? Why do you keep looking for it in the eyes of others?

What if you come
across a dark empty
page in your life?
Can you find all
the possiblities
hiding there?

What if you relax in a
comfortable place and
imagine that you've got
everything you need.
How do you know
that you don't?

What if you are
dreaming now?
Is there anything you
can't do? Why wait
for a dream?

What if you went to
work every day like you
didn't need the money?
Is there a better
way to go?

What if you wear a
tuxedo, evening gown
or nothing at all as you
enter unchartered
territory? Does fate
have a dress code?

What if the best way
to find a full & happy
life is just to be there
for the rest of us?
Can we count on you?

What if bad habits
are just yesterday's
choices? What new
habits can you
choose today?

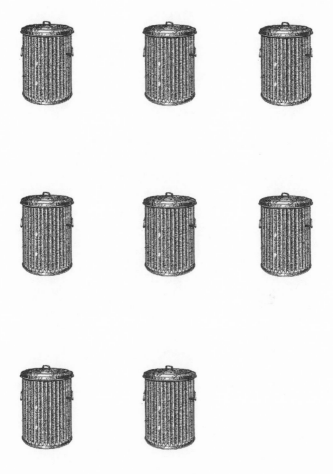

What if you continue
to hurt people you
love? What part of *you*
are you punishing?

What if no one expects
a thing from you?
How many ways can
you surprise them?

What if everything you do each day is just one step in a lifelong work-out? Can you wait until it's over before you look in the mirror?

What if you were to
lose a race or a contest
or a job or a friend
today? How much does
this kind of loss weigh
when you carry it
on your back?

What if being stubborn
is your way of
hiding behind a lack
of conviction? Is it
lonely back there?

What if the quality of your life will only be as good as the quality you bring to this very moment. What kind of moment have you just chosen?

What if you are in a
passionate pursuit of
something or someone?
What missing piece
of you are you
chasing after?

What if the
questions stop?
Where will the
answers come from?

What if you

were to write

the next page?

Or, the next book?

17964106R00113

Made in the USA
Lexington, KY
07 October 2012